She Sleeps on the Water: A Short Collection of Poems

Michele Painter

BookLeaf Publishing

Presentation by *BookLeaf Publishing*

Web: www.bookleafpub.com

E-mail: info@bookleafpub.com

ISBN: 9789357743860

First edition 2023

This book is dedicated to anyone who has ever felt like giving up on life, but is still here to read this...thank you.

The Ocean Called

This is for the sweet ones, with the tender hearts…the strong ones.
Even the Sun and Moon rest on the ocean,
so why don't you?

The ocean called to her and she didn't know why.
How could she?
For inside her heart, she carried a reservoir of tears that even Hercules could not carry.

This reservoir stood anchored deep,
disguised as that self-realized kind of detachment,
but it was nothing but ignored tears cast aside for another time.

When this reservoir became full,
the ocean called to her and she went.

It has occurred to me that the ocean is made of tears,
the kind of tears that are made of love and nothing but That.

Sweet ones, take your tears and dump the contents of your reservoir into the ocean.
You could cry the rest of your life and it would still have room.

You loved and then got hurt.
You got attached. So what?
Please stop hiding your love inside that cross-shaped reservoir you so carefully constructed.
Feel it…I dare you.
For, how can you achieve detachment without first getting to know it?

Don't be afraid of your own love.
When it hurts, take a dip in the ocean,
bathe in all your tears.

Because the tide…this is where grace is found.
It accepts your tears, and if you let it,
it brings your own love back to you in the form of weightless peace.

After you have bathed in your tears and emptied your reservoir,
toss that ugly hiding place into the volcano and let Pele have her way with it.

Do you actually think the Buddha sat under the tree having a great time?
I doubt it.
He probably wept into the Ocean of Consciousness until nothing was left…
except That.

Move Beyond

I am walking through a red mist inside a vibration where You reside
I can hear my soul speaking
What is it telling me?

Where are You?
You are so close
There is so much longing
But why can't I see You?

I must transcend space and time
You are so very near that the past has become the present
The energy of Your touch is still with me...even now
It is beyond my memory
Your blessings are always here

I must transcend the senses
You are right here, but my eyes long to see You
My nose wants to smell Your fragrance
My hands want to touch You
My ears want to hear You whisper in my ear
My tongue wants to taste Your blissful nectar
My entire body wants to feel Your embrace

Oh, my dear mind and senses
You bring me so close and then you separate me again and again
How long will we continue to play this game?

Soon, I must move beyond
For Love has transcended you.

A Piece of Compassion

When I was a young child, my mother and I used to take long walks on the beach.
I would only collect broken shells.
One day she asked me, "Why do you only take the broken ones?"
And I responded, "Because nobody else wants them."

When I was older, she would often tell me this story.
And to this day, no matter how badly I am feeling about myself,
I always know that somewhere inside,
there is a piece of me that contains great compassion.

My question is, "Where is this piece of me?"
Did I give it away?
Was it stolen?
Or, is it simply hidden behind a thick wall of fear bricks that I built inside myself?
I think the latter…

Is it just patiently waiting for me to find it again?

This would make sense,
because compassion never forces its way.
It's too strong for that.

This broken off piece belongs to me.
It's time I go collect it,
let it shine through my eyes again like when I was a child.
How wonderful that would be!

I know a little about fear bricks…
They feel indestructible,
but fear is weak.

Even the tiniest ray of intentional Light could bring down an entire fear wall,
leaving only dust,
which would look so beautiful floating through the Light.

And when that wall comes down,
I will see my own great compassion.
It will be waiting to be picked up off the shore.
And I will say to it,
"No one else has chosen you?
But you are so beautiful!
I will pick you up and take you home,
where you can shine through my eyes once again."

The Power of a Sound

I listened to the strike of a match
It ignited my longing
Its sound vibrations traveled through the space of remembering
Now, I can see who I really am

I perceive the beauty of nature once again
The leaves and the birds carry melodious messages
These vibrations travel from my Heart to your Heart

I hear my Love speaking to me
"I'm right inside the vibrations of your Heart.
Come and rest in me."

Fairy Child

When will I return to the stars?

Speaking to me sweetly
They sparkle into my eyes
And are somehow in my Heart

They speak...
Play with us like when you were a child
We do a playful dance of light upon the forest floor

Swing from those vines that dangle over that creek where the tadpoles are found
Remember that time you finally flew from the trees and into the water?
The exhilaration you felt!

The magic of the stars
The magic of the forest is always with you, Fairy Child
You have always had it in you

Come and play in the lush forest of the Heart
It is waiting for you

For the Heart does not judge how sweet or how mischievous you are
It delights in your curiosity

Explore...
There are hidden places reserved for the creators and thinkers
For the listeners and the ones with prayers
There are special spots in the tree tops for those who need to heal
In the forest, there is a place for everyone
Even you, the one who thought you had nowhere to belong

Play...
The rest will take care of itself
The world will still continue turning
The sun and moon will continue to rise and set

When you get to know the forest
You become one of the fairies
One of the keepers of nature

Remember...
Remember how the forest speaks to you
Remember how you move and dance with us
Stop believing you are paralyzed
Remember...
Come play like when you were a child

So the humans can feel the forest inside themselves again

And as for us, the stars…
We say there is no need to return to somewhere you never left.

Love's Whirlwind

There is a whirlwind of Love inside this body
It is constantly spinning round and round
Where is the ground?

This beautiful storm has made me dizzy with bliss
Laughing, the breeze has inhabited this body so it can dance around with form

Let's be courageous and flow with the grace of the wind
As we inhale Love and exhale Love.

I Found Contentment at the Still Point

One day, I felt lonely and asked for a friend to walk with me.
I was instructed to go meet my new friend at the still point.

"Where can I find the still point?" I asked.
"Follow your breath..."
And so I did.

When I reached the still point, I found a child waiting for me.
"What is your name?" I asked.
"They call me Contentment," she said.

We walked together for a while,
but then I began to run.
Contentment could not keep up.
And for a while I ran without her by my side.

I became exhausted and finally fell down.
In pain, I cried out for help.
At that moment, I saw Contentment walking around the bend.

I became angry and yelled, "Where have you been? I'm in trouble!"

Contentment just smiled and said, "My dear friend, I've been enjoying the company of your breath this whole time. Take a rest, catch your breath and come join me again."

My Breath

My breath...

Moves gracefully and shimmers with iridescent sparks of light
Is a ripple of peaceful, blue silence that is moving and still at the same time
Is within the body and also reaches far beyond it
Grounds me like the love of a mother
Ignites the flame within
Is closer than a lover
Is impassioned and blissful
Slithers like a snake throughout every cell in the body
Has the strength of an Oak that stands strong without muscles
Is all the stars in the sky
Moves up and down like a blade of grass that grows tall and then withers
Travels to secret places
Plays hide-and-seek
Is connected to my mind and emotions but also completely free

My breath moves within the universe

And the entire universe is within...

My breath...

Your Laughter

What's this!?
I'm quite certain I can hear You laughing
Your laughter is ringing in my ear
It's busy resonating and penetrating every part of my being
It won't miss a single cell
From deep inside me, Your laughter is coming from its source
It's calling me to come and play
So, I will follow the sound of Your laughter back to the source of laughter itself...
My Self!

In a Single Flame

In the darkness of the early morning
In private
You ignited a fire within me

First, it was a tiny flame

Then

It grew
and grew
and grew

Until the entire world was engulfed in flames
I climbed the last tree standing and watched the world burn in Love

Then

Everything became one
The entire universe was suddenly contained in a single flame

I held this flame in the palm of my hand and waved it before You

I could see You smile sweetly as You watched it dancing around

Dancing around
In Your praise.

The Love Story of Michele

Learning to love ourselves can be a messy process.
And by "messy" I mean deeply wounding and healing.
This is the case with Michele.

She ripped her heart to bloody shreds,
left herself barely alive in a pool of her own fear.
Why did she do this?
Because she was afraid to love herself.

She's also dropped everything to save her own life.
The way a best friend would - no questions asked.
Why did she do this?
Because she chose to love herself.

How can you just walk away from that,
pretend nothing happened?
You can't...

After saving herself she began to realize,

that maybe she was actually worth saving after all.

Slowly, Michele gathered the pieces of her heart and began to put them back together,
like the most important puzzle that ever existed.
In her own ways, she began to heal.

She began reaching out to others so she wouldn't have to mend alone.
And there came a time, when Michele had enough strength to stand on her own two feet again.

This is forgiveness and humility in action.
This is learning to love one's self,
and it is learning to trust.

It's a process.
I believe Michele has reached a point where it doesn't have to look so brutal anymore.
Maybe she can begin to enjoy this process a little more,
face her fears more gracefully and express her love more tenderly.

She is a best friend, a student of life, a passionate lover and beautifully unique.
She is not meant to navigate life alone.

This is the love story of Michele,
and it’s a beautiful one.

Lost and Found in a Dream

The room went dark and we were covered by black veils.
We needed to stay hidden in order to survive.
Accompanying me was an old decrepit woman.
She stood hunched over, sad and pathetic looking.
I found myself repulsed by her,
but under the circumstances remained by her side.

Another woman in the room whispered in my ear,
"There are demons in this temple."
I whispered back,
"I know, I can feel it."
I began to pray,
and then awoke.

Eleven years later,
I re-entered this dream as my present self.

This time, I was not afraid and I wanted to meet the decrepit old woman.
I wanted to look into her eyes.

I walked over to her and gently pulled back her
veil.

To my surprise, a sweet, angelic little girl
walked out of the darkness.
Her spirit was strong, shined bright and she was
happy to see me.
I picked her up and told her everything was
safe.
She clung to me as I carried her out of the
dream,
and far away from our demons.

I needed her too.

Rose Petals of Light

There are rose petals of light within every corner of the mind
Waiting to unfold
Break free
And spread fragrance all over our awareness

Let them have their fun
And forget your worries.

She Is

She is my Beloved
I cannot resist Her any longer
I open up to a fresh awareness of Her presence inside me
My breath takes me closer and closer
The energy of Her love is vibrating within me
Her bliss is spilling out everywhere
She is caressing me softly as She takes me to places unknown
I want to trust Her
I want to offer myself completely to Her
She is my Beloved
She is Grace.

The Perfect Storm

There is a sudden hush of anticipation
The wind has become still
Listen...
The perfect storm is here

I watch as this storm moves the entire universe
It tears down walls
And destroys everything in its path

I stand in the eye of this perfect storm and observe the destruction in silence
I stand in the eye of this perfect storm and see a pathway unfurl in front of me
I stand in the eye of this perfect storm and all obstacles are washed away
I stand in the eye of this perfect storm and am escorted to a brand new threshold

I melt into the eye of this perfect storm as it brings me back to You.

The Old Man

I sat one day and turned my eyes inward.
There, I saw an old man walking down a very long road toward the setting sun.
I approached him and asked him who he was.
And he answered, “I am you.”

“You are my soul?” I asked.
He nodded his head to confirm.
“I never thought my soul would come to me looking like an old man.”
We both chuckled.

I continued to ask him questions, and he always gave me an answer.
I thanked him for being my friend and I left him to continue walking.

Every now and then, I check in with him.
Sometimes he is strong and some days he is weak and can barely move forward.
One day, I held him up and helped him walk.
Another day, he carried me.

He always tells me the truth about myself.
And he always keeps moving toward the light,
even if it’s at a snail's pace.

The Fountain of Youth

I visited the Fountain of Youth.
I drank its water.
It did not make me younger.

Instead the fountain told me to pray,
send well wishes.
For, prayers are not bound by time as we know it.
After we die our prayers continue to carry our loved ones for eternity.

It is also good to pray for those who have passed.
After all, their souls are still alive and well.

So, pray for those you love,
and for those you hate.
Pray for the living and the dead.
Pray for the earth, wind, sun and moon.
Pray for all living things, including yourself.
And pray for the spirits who watch over us.

Men have wasted their lives searching for the Fountain of Youth...
But all we need to do is pray.

Sparkles of Light

Oh, Sparkles of Light on the Water

You refresh my spirit
You are gentle and kind
I look at You, and without a mirror, I can see the twinkle in my own eyes
You are so still and yet so quick
You are a wonderful mystery to me
You are born out of the union between sunlight and water...light and dark
You are the stillness at the end of each exhale
And somehow, You also exist in the breeze against my face
You carry messages and blessings into my view
You exist so that I can enjoy You
And now, I am praising You.

Dear Grandpa

Dear Grandpa,

I wish I had gotten to know you,
wish I could go back in time,
when you were in the back yard that day,
deciding whether or not to pull the trigger.

Since I can't time travel, I will write you a letter
now.
May your spirit receive it...

When it comes to life, people often say that
giving up is not an option.
But that's not true is it?
We both know that.
You're a perfect example of the choices we
have.

I don't say this with anger.
I've heard a little about what you saw and
experienced during your life,
and I understand if you were tired of fighting.

My mother told me you would never speak of
your time in Germany.

I wish that you would have talked about it or written about it.
You suffered in silence and that makes me sad.

Over twenty years after you left us,
a fellow soldier of yours wrote letters to your children.
These letters told them the stories you always refused to speak about.

He told them about how you saved his life against orders,
while grenades went off around you,
how you wouldn't leave him,
carried him back to the helicopter and saved his life.
He told your children that you were his hero.

He told them about how you helped shut down concentration camps.
I can't imagine the things you must have seen,
but I can imagine that you saved many lives.

I know you must have been so exhausted,
but why didn't you save your own life?

You have many grandchildren and great grandchildren.
We know what a good man you were.

I have never heard anyone say a bad word about you.

I have felt like giving up on life before too.
I wish you would have been here for me to talk to during those times.
You would have understood.
Feeling that someone understands you is rare and priceless.

I want to help us,
all the souls in our family who have been cursed with the urge to give up on life.

First, I will do everything I can to heal myself.
Then, I will take an inner journey...
a journey to meet our demons face to face.
I'll fight a battle for us just like you did for many people.
God help me I'll come out alive,
heads of those demons in my hands,
toss them into the fire of Love,
watch them burn...

The smoke will rise and heal us all.

Grandpa, I want to do this for our family,
but I can't do it alone.
I need to ask you to fight one more battle.

We'll do it together,
heal this pain once and for all.

Love you.

The Eulogy of Every Day

There was this girl I knew
Every day she would heal a little
And every day she would die a little

The more she healed, the more she died
But she didn't mind
It's what she came to do

Her eyes were the same as the stars
But she often forgot...
And then sometimes remembered

She would always get excited at the first signs of Spring
You know, when the tulips start budding
And the geese start coming

She would wonder how the delicate sea foam formed
Not realizing she was born from it

She would get lost in music
Dream of being magical
Even though she already was

She was gentle and unassuming
Underestimated
By others
And herself

People both praised and scorned her quietude
And when she would speak her opinion...mostly scorn

She saw it had been normalized to feel one way and act another
She walked around in everyone's lies, including her own
It was empty there

She knew people mostly heard only what they wanted
And she often preferred conversing with the trees
For, they knew how to listen and how to be seen

She would pick flowers
Only to watch them die a little each day
But she would also praise them for their beauty all along the way

At sunset
She would feel a little less alive
But somehow a little more whole

She would go to bed every night
Wake up every morning
And then discover who she was today

For, she wasn't the same girl as yesterday.

She Sleeps on the Water

Everyday I wait...

She slowly rises up out of the ocean
Her light dancing upon the surface of the water

The birds become still in Her presence
The crickets sing praise to this Goddess

Night comes...

My eyes absorb Her glowing complexion
My ears take delight in Her magical silence
I feel Her energy move through my body
Spiraling and undulating

I enter the water and bathe in the glow of Her light
I enjoy Her gentle caress on my skin

I find Her inside me
She soothes loneliness and reveals the ecstasy of the soul
Content, I fall into a dream state while wrapped in Her safe embrace

Dawn approaches...

I stand on the shore
And watch Her vanish into the water where She sleeps
She is a mystery to my mind

When my time comes...

And all separation has vanished
I will sleep with Her in complete fullness as lovers should.

Printed in the USA
CPSIA information can be obtained
at www.ICGtesting.com
LVHW080749051123
763047LV00076B/1644

9 789357 743860